The LET'S FIND OUT Books

by Martha and Charles Shapp

LET'S FIND OUT ABOUT AIR
LET'S FIND OUT WHAT'S BIG AND WHAT'S SMALL
LET'S FIND OUT ABOUT COWBOYS
LET'S FIND OUT WHAT ELECTRICITY DOES
LET'S FIND OUT ABOUT FIREMEN
LET'S FIND OUT ABOUT HOUSES
LET'S FIND OUT ABOUT INDIANS
LET'S FIND OUT WHAT'S LIGHT AND WHAT'S HEAVY
LET'S FIND OUT ABOUT POLICEMEN
LET'S FIND OUT ABOUT SCHOOL
LET'S FIND OUT WHAT THE SIGNS SAY
LET'S FIND OUT WHAT'S IN THE SKY
LET'S FIND OUT ABOUT THE UNITED NATIONS
LET'S FIND OUT ABOUT WATER
LET'S FIND OUT ABOUT WHEELS

and

LET'S FIND OUT ABOUT SPRING
LET'S FIND OUT ABOUT SUMMER
LET'S FIND OUT ABOUT FALL
LET'S FIND OUT ABOUT WINTER

LET'S FIND OUT ABOUT

AIR

by

MARTHA AND CHARLES SHAPP

Pictures by László Roth

FRANKLIN WATTS, INC.
575 Lexington Avenue, New York 22

Library of Congress Catalog Card Number: 63-14685
Printed in the United States of America
by The Moffa Press

1   2   3   4   5

You need air to live.
Animals need air to live.

All living things need air.

The air you need is all around you.
The air is everywhere.
You can't see air.

It has no color.
It has no shape.
But it is there.

Push a dry piece of paper to the bottom of a glass.

Put the glass into water.
Take the glass out of the water.

Take the paper out of the glass.

The paper is dry.
The air in the glass keeps the water out.

There is air in the holes of a sponge.
Put a sponge into water.

Squeeze the sponge.
The air comes out of the sponge in bubbles.

There is air in soil.
The tiny spaces in soil are filled with air.
Put some dry soil into a pan.

Pour water on the soil.
The air in the tiny spaces is pushed out by the water.
The air comes out in bubbles.

Run with a piece of cardboard.

You can feel the cardboard pushing against something.
It is pushing against air.

Run with a small, flat paper bag.
The bag fills up with air.

Air does many things for you.
You ride on air.

The air in tires makes the ride smoother.

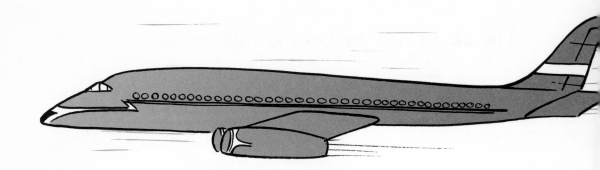

Airplanes ride on air.
Air keeps airplanes up.

You can play with air.
The ball you bounce is filled with air.

The wind is moving air.
The wind takes kites up and keeps them flying high.

Soap bubbles are bubbles of air.
When you blow soap bubbles, you
are blowing air.

Air helps to make music.
Blow air in and out it comes with music.

Air cleans the house.
Moving air pushes dirt into the cleaner.

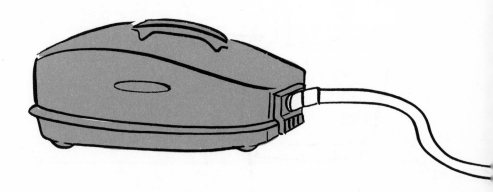

U. S. 1224595

Moving air keeps you cool.

Air makes things float.
Put a balloon into a pan of water.
It sinks to the bottom.

Blow up the balloon and tie it closed.
Put the blown-up balloon into the water.
It floats!

You can't see air.
But it's all around you — everywhere.

VOCABULARY LIST (95 Words)

a
against
air
airplanes
all
and
animals
are
around

bag
ball
balloon
blow(ing)
blown-up
bottom
bounce
bubbles
but
by

can('t)
cardboard
clean (er) (s)
closed
color
comes
cool

dirt
does
dry

everywhere

feel
fill (ed) (s)
flat

float(s)
flying
for

glass

has
helps
high
holes
house

in
into
is
it('s)

keeps
kites

live
living

make(s)
many
moving
music

need
no

of
on
out

pan
paper
piece

play
pour
push (ed) (es) (ing)
put

ride
run

see
shape
sinks
small
smoother
soap
soil
some
something
spaces
sponge
squeeze

take(s)
the
them
there
things
tie
tiny
tires
to

up

water
when
wind
with

you